KU-726-472

Published simultaneously in 1995 by Exley Publications in Great Britain, and Exley
Giftbooks in the USA.

12  11  10  9  8  7  6  5  4  3  2

**Copyright © Helen Exley 1995**

**ISBN 1-85015-641-7**

A copy of the CIP data is available from the British Library on request.

Edited and pictures selected by Helen Exley.
Designed by Pinpoint Design Company.
Pictures researched by P. A. Goldberg and J. M. Clift, Image Select, London.
Typesetting by Delta, Watford.
Printed in Singapore.
**Exley Publications Ltd, 16 Chalk Hill, Watford, Herts WDl 4BN, United Kingdom.**
**Exley Giftbooks, 232 Madison Avenue, Suite 1206, New York, NY 10016, USA.**

Acknowledgements: The publishers are grateful for permission to reproduce
copyright material. While every effort has been made to trace copyright holders, the
publishers would be pleased to hear from any not here acknowledged.
James Baldwin: extract from "Go Tell It On The Mountain" © 1952, 1953 by James
Baldwin. Used by permission of Doubleday, a division of Bantam, Doubleday, Dell
Publishing Group; A.S.Byatt: extract from "Still Life" published by Chatto and
Windus. Reprinted by permission of Chatto and Windus, Scribner, a division of
Simon and Schuster, Inc. from "Still Life" © 1985 A.S.Byatt and The Peters, Fraser
and Dunlop Group Ltd; Noel Coward: extract from "Remembered Laughter",
published by Jonathan Cape on behalf of The Estate of Noel Coward; Anna
Quindlen: extract from The New York Times © 1986 by The New York Times
Company. Reprinted by permission.
Picture Credits: Exley Publications is very grateful to the following individuals and
organizations for permission to reproduce their pictures : Alinari Archive (AA),
Archiv Für Kunst (AKG), Art Resource (AR), The Bridgeman Art Library (BAL),
Christie's Images (CI ), Edimedia (EDM), Fine Art Photographic Library Ltd (FAP),
Image Bank (IB), Scala (SCA) Cover: F . W . Bourdillon "Jubilee Hat ", Private
Collection ( BAL); title page: Alfred Edward Emslie (FAP); page 7: © 1995 Margaret
Gere (1878-1965) "Little Boy Asleep", The Fine Art Society, London (BAL); page 9:
Thomas Davidson (FAP); page 11: © 1995 Sir William Rothenstein (1872-1945)
"Mother and Child", Cheltenham Art Gallery and Museums, Glos (BAL); page 13:
Fratelli Tkaciov (SCA); page 15: Frederick Bacon Barwell (FAP); page 16: © 1995
Hans Baluschek (1870-1935) "The Emigrés", Markisches Museum, Berlin (AKG);
page 18: Anonymous (FAP); page 21: Michelangelo (AR/SCA); page 23: Le Nain
(BLZ); page 25: Mark Graham (IB); page 27: Jonathan Eastman Johnson (AKG); page
29: Claude Monet (EDM); page 30: © 1995 Jessica Hayllar (1858-1940) "Autumn
Sunlight" (FAP); page 32: El Greco (AKG); page 35: G. Pellizza (AA); page 37:
Niccolo Cannicci (SCA); page 38: Alexander M. Rossi (FAP); page 41: Edward
Robert Hughes, Chris Beetles Ltd, London (BAL); page 43: Amedeo Modigliani,
National Gallery of Art, Washington D.C. (BAL); page 45: Anders Zorn (AKG); page
46: Graugaise (EDM); page 48: George Morton (FAP); page 50: Andrej Jakowlew
(AKG); page 52: (AKG); page 55: Charles Ernest Butler (FAP); page 57: William Lee-
Hankey, Oldham Art Gallery, Lancs (BAL); page 58: Elizabeth Stanhope Forbes,
Whitford and Hughes, London (BAL); page 61: Vincenzo Caprile ( SCA).

# THE LOVE BETWEEN
# *Mothers and Sons*

EDITED BY

H E L E N   E X L E Y

**EXLEY**
NEW YORK • WATFORD, UK

"It's such a powerful connection;
it takes me by surprise. I feel
like there's a dotted line
connecting me to my son."

SARAH LANGSTON

"Romance fails us and so do
friendships but the relationship of
Mother and Child remains indelible
and indestructible – the strongest bond
upon this earth."

THEODOR REIK

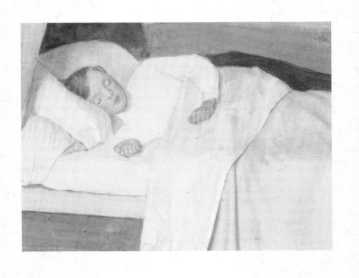

"There is an enduring tenderness in the love of a mother to a son that transcends all other affections of the heart. It is neither to be chilled by selfishness, nor daunted by danger, nor weakened by worthlessness, nor stifled by ingratitude. She will sacrifice every comfort to his convenience; she will surrender every pleasure to his enjoyment; she will glory in his fame and exalt in his prosperity; and if adversity overtake him, he will be the dearer to her by misfortune; and if disgrace settle upon his name, she will still love and cherish him; and if all the world beside cast him off, she will be all the world to him."

**WASHINGTON IRVING (1783-1859)**

"He would sit on her knee and look at her face, testing her contours with fingers that in the early days, judging distances, jabbed at a bright eye or clawed at a lip-corner, and grew rapidly skilled at caressing, patting her cheek, tangling her hair. She saw herself in him: the learning face was her face. They looked into each other's eyes and she saw herself reflected, a looming light, a loving moon, part of himself? His flesh was her flesh...."

A. S. BYATT, b.1936, FROM "STILL LIFE"

"The child, in the decisive first years of his life, has the experience of his mother, as an all-enveloping, protective nourishing power. Mother is food; she is love; she is warmth; she is earth. To be loved by her means to be alive, to be rooted, to be at home."

**ERICH FROMM (1900-1980)**

"Nobody can have the soul of me. My mother has had it, and nobody can have it again. Nobody can come into my very self again, and breathe me in like an atmosphere."

D. H. LAWRENCE (1885-1930)

"To my mother I tell the truth. I have no thought, no feeling that I cannot share with my mother, and she is like a second conscience to me, her eyes like a mirror reflecting my own image."

WILLIAM GERHARDI (1895-1977)

"Probably there is nothing in human nature more resonant with charges than the flow of energy between two biologically alike bodies, one of which has lain in amniotic bliss inside the other, one of which has labored to give birth to the other."

ADRIENNE RICH, b.1939

"A child's hand in yours – what tenderness it arouses, what power it conjures. You are instantly the very touchstone of wisdom and strength."

MARJORIE HOLMES,
FROM "CALENDAR OF LOVE AND
INSPIRATION"


"What feeling is so nice as a child's hand in yours? So small, so soft and warm, like a kitten huddling in the shelter of your clasp."

MARJORIE HOLMES,
FROM "CALENDAR OF LOVE AND
INSPIRATION"

*"My child looked at me and I looked back at him in the delivery room, and I realized that out of a sea of infinite possibilities it had come down to this: a specific person, born on the hottest day of the year, conceived on a Christmas Eve, made by his father and me miraculously from scratch."*

**ANNA QUINDLEN,
FROM "NEW YORK TIMES",
MARCH 13, 1986**

"Mothers don't really have premonitions. They have been over every possible eventuality so often – both good and ill – that *whatever* happens to you, they've rehearsed it."

PAM BROWN, b.1928

"My mother always phones me and asks, 'Is everything all wrong?'"

RICHARD LEWIS

"If a child is to keep alive his inborn
sense of wonder he needs the
companionship of at least one adult
who can share it, rediscovering with
him the joy, excitement and mystery
of the world we live in."

RACHEL CARSON (1907-1964)

"'You getting to be,' she said, putting her hand beneath his chin and holding his face away from her, 'a right big boy. You going to be a mighty fine man, you know that? Your mamma's counting on you.' And he knew again that she was not saying everything she meant; in a kind of secret language she was telling him something that he must remember and understand tomorrow. He watched her face, his heart swollen with love for her and with an anguish, not yet his own, that he did not understand and that frightened him. 'Yes, Ma,' he said, hoping that she would realize, despite his stammering tongue, the depth of his passion to please her."

JAMES BALDWIN (1924-1987),
FROM "GO TELL IT ON THE MOUNTAIN"

"...the walks and talks we have with our
two-year-olds in red boots have a great
deal to do with the values they will
cherish as adults."

**EDITH F. HUNTER, b.1919**

*In a child's lunch basket,*
*a mother's thoughts.*

**JAPANESE PROVERB**

"In the effort to give good and comforting answers to the young questioners whom we love, we very often arrive at good and comforting answers for ourselves."

RUTH GOODE

"I showed you the world through my eyes. Now you show it to me through yours. And so we learn."

PAM BROWN, b.1928

"Your first butterfly. Your first rainbow. Your first dinosaur. In sharing your childhood I relived my own."

PAM BROWN, b.1928

"We bear the world, and we make it.... There was never a great man who had not a great mother – it is hardly an exaggeration."

OLIVE SCHREINER (1855-1920)

"Every breath she ever breathed, every effort she ever made, every prayer she ever prayed was for her son.... The greatest break that Francis Albert Sinatra ever enjoyed in his entire life, in his entire career, was to have Dolly as a mother."

REVEREND ROBERT PERELLA

"Everybody knows that a good mother gives her children a feeling of trust and stability.... Somehow even her clothes feel different to her children's hands from anybody else's clothes. Only to touch her skirt or her sleeve makes a troubled child feel better."

KATHARINE BUTLER
HATHAWAY

"Children, look into those eyes, listen to the dear voice, notice the feeling of even a single touch that is bestowed upon you by that gentle hand! Make much of it while yet you have that most precious of all good gifts, – a loving mother. Read the unfathomable love of those eyes; the kind anxiety of that tone and look, however slight your pain. In after life you may have friends, fond, dear friends, but never will you have again the inexpressible love and gentleness lavished upon you, which none but mother bestows."

THOMAS BABINGTON MACAULAY
(1800-1859)

"Fifty-four years of love and tenderness
and crossness and devotion and unswerving
loyalty. Without her I could only have
achieved a quarter of what I have achieved,
not only in terms of success and career,
but in terms of personal happiness. We have
quarrelled, often violently, over the years,
but she has never stood between me and
my life, never tried to hold me too tightly,
always let me go free. For a woman of her
strength of character this was truly remarkable....
There was no fear in her except for me.
She was a great woman to whom I owe the
whole of my life."

NÖEL COWARD (1899-1973)

"How many thousands of heroines there must be now, of whom we shall never know. But still they are there. They sow in secret the seed of which we pluck the flower, and eat the fruit, and know not that we pass the sower daily in the streets. One form of heroism – the most common, and yet the least remembered of all – namely, the heroism of the average mother. Ah! When I think of that broad fact, I gather hope again for poor humanity; and this dark world looks bright – this diseased world looks wholesome to me once more – because, whatever else it is not full of, it is at least full of mothers."

**CHARLES KINGSLEY (1819-1875)**

"Who is it that loves me and will love me for ever with an affection which no chance, no misery, no crime of mine can do away? It is you, my mother."

THOMAS CARLYLE (1795-1881),
IN A LETTER TO HIS MOTHER, AUGUST 29, 1824

"The God to whom little boys say their prayers has a face very like their mother's."

JAMES M. BARRIE (1860-1937)

*"A happy childhood is one
of the best gifts that parents
have in their power to
bestow."*

R. CHOLMONDELEY

*"If you make children
happy now, you will make
them happy twenty years
hence by the memory of it."*

**KATE DOUGLAS WIGGIN**
**(1856-1953)**

"She (mother) was so deeply imbedded in my
consciousness that for the first year of school I
seem to have believed that each of my teachers
was my mother in disguise."

PHILIP ROTH, b.1933,
FROM "PORTNOY'S COMPLAINT"

"Parents, however old they
and we may grow to be,
serve among other things to
shield us from a sense of
our doom. As long as they
are around, we can avoid
the fact of
our mortality; we can still
be innocent children."

ELIZABETH JANE HOWARD, b.1923,
FROM "A DIFFERENT WOMAN"

"In the sheltered simplicity of the first days after a baby is born, one sees again the magical closed circle, the miraculous sense of two people existing only for each other."

ANNE MORROW LINDBERGH, b.1906

"In his mother's heart no baby ever grows up completely and in some mysterious fashion a part of every man remains a child, peculiarly his mother's, even though they are estranged. In that case there is sorrow for them both but whatever sense of hurt or injustice a man may harbour, he knows, in the depth of his soul, that his mother is waiting always for his return."

DAME ENID LYONS

"A mother's love for the child of her body differs essentially from all other affections, and burns with so steady and clear a flame that it appears like the one unchangeable thing in this earthly mutable life, so that when she is no longer present it is still a light to our steps and a consolation."

W. H. HUDSON (1841-1922)

Thou, straggler into loving arms,
Young climber-up of knees,
When I forget thy thousand ways
Then life and all shall cease.

MARY LAMB (1764-1847)


You too, my mother, read my rhymes
For love of unforgotten times,
And you may chance
to hear once more
The little feet along the floor.

ROBERT LOUIS STEVENSON (1850-1894)

*"Do you remember – winter mornings, dark and cold and rustling? The first day away, walking to a shining sea and the sound of gulls? Lopsided birthday cakes? Walks through spring woods? I do, I do."*

PAM BROWN, b.1928

*"Sons are the anchors of a mother's life."*

SOPHOCLES (496-406 B.C.),
FROM "PHAEDRA"


*"I love his laugh,...it bubbles out in an infectious
wholehearted way. This is pure joy – nothing
else matters."*

ANNE MORROW LINDBERGH, b.1906